DEEP ROOTS

Here is a list of the books I have written:

Little Chase & Big Fat Aunt May
Little Chase & Big Fat Aunt May Ride Again
Little Chase & Big Fat Aunt May Cookbook
Son of Immigrants: James M. Imahara
A Tourist's Guide to West Feliciana
The Travels of Baby Stewart
Audubon Plantation Country Cookbook (Pelican Pub.)
Bayou Plantation Country Cookbook (Pelican Pub.)
Acadiana Plantation Country Cookbook (Pelican Pub.)
River Road Plantation Country Cookbook (Pelican Pub.)
Louisiana Swamp Tours (Pelican Publ.)
Lost and Found at the Plantation Bed & Breakfast
The Herman and Little Leon Stories
Pelican Guide to Louisiana Plantations (edit) (Pelican Pub.)
Angola: Louisiana State Penitentiary (UL Press)
Dying To Tell (UL Press)
Weep For The Living (Pelican Pub.)
Louisiana Highway One (UL Press)
Main Streets of Louisiana (UL Press)
Louisiana's Swamps & Marshes: Easy Access (UL Press)
The Ivorybill Hotel
St. Francisville & West Feliciana Parish: Images of America
(Arcadia Press)
Bayou Sara (UL Press)
Big Badass Boar Cookbook

DEEP ROOTS

The Story of a Place and Its People

Anne Butler

Cover Images: Kathleen Harris.
Colonel George Mathews in 1777 leading the 9th Virginia Regiment at the Revolutionary War Battle of Brandywine, partial reproduction of "The Nation Makers" painted in 1902 by Howard Pyle; original at Brandywine Museum.

Hope Estate Plantation, ca. 1855, by Marie Adrien Persac, LSU Museum of Art, Gift of the Friends of the LSU Museum of Art. Photography: Kim Jones.

Print information available on the last page.

Rev. date: 07/06/2018

To order additional copies of this book, contact:
Xlibris
1-888-795-4274
www.Xlibris.com
Orders@Xlibris.com
781622

Contents

FOREWORD

Once, when I was conducting a tour through the historic Butler Greenwood Plantation house where I have lived for more than half a century, a man entered and immediately burst into tears. I asked what was wrong, and he answered, "It smells just like my grandmother's house." He probably meant a mixture of wood smoke and mold and lavender sachet. And he was right. It smelled like the past, like history, like family stories repeated over and over by every generation, growing in grandeur with every telling.

I'm not a professional genealogist, nor do I consider myself a real historian. What I am is a storyteller, an author whose works are accessible, easy to read, not cluttered with footnotes and references (in other words, they give real authentic historians nightmares). My specialty is taking a million disparate bits and pieces, undated unattributed flotsam and jetsam, yellowing newspaper clippings and tattered journals, fading photos and diminishing memories, and putting them all together into a cohesive whole.

There's a quote on some genealogy site referencing those chosen in each family to be the storytellers of the tribe, to find the ancestors and put flesh on their bones and make them seem alive again, to tell the family story, to breathe life into all who have gone before.

And I thought to myself, "If I don't write this history and these family stories down, they are going to be lost." And so I did what I do best. I wrote.

THE FIRST GENERATION

Dr. Samuel Flower and his wife Mary Carpenter

Dr. Samuel Flower (1751-1813) and Mary Carpenter (1760-1812)

The pacifist physician Samuel Flower was the first of the family to set foot in Louisiana, descending from a Norman ancestor first given the name LeFleur for his physical beauty, but as a Quaker, the presumably modest Dr. Flower would no doubt have nightmares to see how his descendants pride themselves on their looks. One distinguished gentleman of a later generation of the family was disparaged by a competing early pioneer as "vain as a peacock and ugly as an owl," although his portrait actually shows a very handsome visage. It would no doubt give Dr. Flower even more pains to learn of the subsequent generations marrying into the Mathews family, one of whom survived being bayoneted some nine times in the Revolutionary War, and even worse, into the Butler family of brave warriors fighting battles alongside George Washington and Andrew Jackson; one who was tomahawked to death during the Indian Wars even had his heart eaten to pass on his bravery. And once the Episcopal Church had been established here in 1827, with a Flower and several Butlers on the very first vestry, by the second generation they were suddenly all staunch Episcopalians, the Quaker never being heard of again.

From *The History of Chester and its Vicinity: Chronicles of the Early Flower Family* as well as letters, some of which are accurate and some not, we learn that the Flower family of Chester, Pennsylvania, dated its origin from the Norman Conquest. Hugh, one of the adventurers that gathered under the standard of the Duke of Normandy when he announced his intention of invading England, received the name of LeFleur (which in time came to be translated as Flower) "from his most remarkable beauty and his valourous conduct on the field of battle" according to Layfair's "Noble Families of England.

First to arrive in America was William Flower, who settled in Marcus Hook in 1692; he was a Quaker, son of Enoch Flower who had purchased 2000 acres of land from William Penn. William's daughter Mary married John Flower, son or grandson of Sir Charles Flower, said to have been the Lord Mayor of London. Earlier generations in England had served in parliament and been knighted.

Colonel Benjamin Flower (1748-1781) was a friend of General George Washington, serving during the Revolutionary War as Commisary of the Military Stores. He was said to have been responsible for hiding the Liberty Bell when the British routed Washington in the battles of Brandywine and Germantown; supposedly he took the bell from Philadelphia and concealed it in Allentown Reformed Church. This comes from a chart in the Flag House in Baltimore. Benjamin's sister Rebecca Flower married William Young and had a daughter Mary Young Pickersgill whose flag shop in Baltimore was commissioned to make the flag that flew over Fort McHenry, which came under siege by a British fleet during the War of 1812. This was the flag that inspired Francis Scott Key's *Star Spangled Banner*; it had 15 stars and stripes, and she was paid $405.90 for it.

Dr. Samuel Flower was the son of Samuel Sr., a wealthy Justice of the Peace who could afford an in-house tutor for his children, and Rebecca Branson, also from a very wealthy family. The Bransons were owners of the most important forge in Pennsylvania, called Windsor Forge, in Lancaster, and Rebecca inherited shares in the forge from her grandfather William Branson.

Samuel Flower came south from Pennsylvania in 1773 while the area was under British control. Louisiana had first been claimed by France, but when France lost the rest of the area to Spain, the vast territory east of the Mississippi went to England in 1763 and was known as West Florida. The seat of government for British West Florida was Pensacola, and the last British governor (1770-1781) was Governor Peter Chester. The tiny hamlet where Baton Rouge is located now was called by the British Richmond or New Richmond.

The British fortification there, Fort New Richmond, was hastily constructed on a commandeered portion of Dr. Flower's original plantation, and there are British Parliament entreaties to repay the owners of the plantation for the loss of their land. The plantation, called Belmont, was co-owned with Stephen Watts, Pennsylvania-born descendent of Sir Thomas Watts, Lord Mayor of London in 1600. His wife Frances Assheton was a member of a distinguished Quaker family with close associations to William Penn, and Thomas Assheton was married to Dr. Samuel Flower's sister Hannah. An attorney, Stephen Watts moved to Louisiana in the early 1770s and became Recorder of Deeds of the English settlement on the

Mississippi River, as well as Justice of the Quorum and King's Attorney for the District of British New Richmond.

This New Richmond fortification became the Spanish Fort San Carlos, rebuilt and greatly improved, during the Revolutionary War after the governor of Spanish Louisiana, Bernardo de Galvez, in 1779 ousted the British from that portion of West Florida he called Feliciana. In the fall of 1810, this was the site of the Republic of West Florida's successful attack and overthrow of the Spanish regime; Mary Carpenter Flower's brother James was a participant in this rebellion against Spanish claims to continue control of the area east of the Mississippi River even after the 1803 Louisiana Purchase.

Samuel Flower and Mary Carpenter were wed in 1777. The original wedding certificate, sealed with wax and witnessed by Stephen Watts, Joseph Carpenter, Ruth Carpenter, Frances Watts, Elizabeth Carpenter, Richard Carpenter and several others, says, *"To whom it may concern: This is to certify that on the fourteenth day of June in the year of our Lord one thousand seven hundred and seventy seven, by virtue of a special license from his excellency Governor Chester I did in presence of the underwritten whose names are subscribed as witnesses join together in the holy state of matrimony (there being no clergyman in the place) Samuel Flower Esquire and Miss Mary Carpenter according to the rites and ceremonies of the church of England there being no lawful course to obstruct the same consistent with my knowledge In testimony whereof I have here unto subscribed my name and affixed my seal the day and year first above written at Richmond."*

The wedding of Samuel Flower and Mary Carpenter took place at the Quaker Meeting House on her father Richard Carpenter's 2000-acre plantation 4 miles below Baton Rouge; during his ownership, from the late 1760s to 1785, he built a large home, a store and also a Friend's Meeting House, its architecture very different from the main house with a Gothic window and central chimney. There were only a handful of Quakers in the area at this time, and the Meeting House would later be consecrated as the first Catholic Church in the area around 1790. He also improved the land and planted indigo. The third owner of Carpenter's house called it Hope Estate and remodeled it around 1820 with additions shown in a Marie Adrien Persac painting; the original of this watercolor is in the LSU Art Museum.

Richard Carpenter, Mary C. Flower's father by his first wife Ruth Collins, had moved from Rhode Island to Pensacola (1765-1769), was a sea captain and ran a mercantile house. He served on the governing council of British West Florida during this time, and represented his brother-in-law, Rhode Island governor John Collins, who owned a large trading firm. According to one source, he received land grants in 1768 of 10,000 acres on the Alabama River above Mobile and 2,000 acres below New Richmond (later Baton Rouge).

In the mid-1780s Richard Carpenter moved to the Natchez District of Spanish West Florida and was the pre-eminent merchant in that area, with hundreds of debtors at the time of his death in 1788 and an estate which was valued at $50,000. Dr. Samuel Flower was an executor for the estate; Carpenter had died at Flower's home. In Richard Carpenter's will, he leaves 800 acres granted to him by the government to his son James with the intent that a house be built "for the reception of my wife and family;" to his beloved wife Mary he left "a negro man 'Boston,' negro woman 'Anny,' and all the furniture," plus 12 cows and calves and his white horse; he later changed this bequest so that 4 cows and calves went to his wife and the remaining 8 cows and calves to his youngest children, both minors at the time, James only 8 and Sarah 11 months. His house and lot "at Natchez landing" was to be sold, plus 300 acres, the profits after paying all debts to be divided among his son and three daughters. After a spirited auction, Stephen Minor would purchase both the house and lot in Natchez for $3100 and the plantation for $300.

After the death in 1770 of his first wife Ruth, with whom he had two daughters who survived to adulthood (including Mary, who married Dr. Samuel Flower) and four sons who died as infants, Richard Carpenter had married Mary Fairchild, widow of Daniel Lewis who drowned in the Mississippi River while taking a raft-load of supplies downriver. With Daniel Lewis, Mary had three sons, one by the name of Seth Lewis; with Richard Carpenter, she had two children who survived, James and Sarah, who would become the first wife of Judge George Mathews whose second wife would be Harriett Flower, daughter of Dr. Samuel Flower and his wife Mary Carpenter. Mary Fairchild Lewis Carpenter would survive her husband and marry yet again, in 1804, to Governor George Mathews, father of Judge George Mathews who had married her daughter Sarah.

Samuel Flower had also moved to Natchez, Mississippi, in 1785 after the British loss of New Richmond. There he was the well-respected personal doctor to Governor Manuel Gayosa de Lemos. Don Manuel Gayoso de Lemos, a Brigadier General, served as District Governor of the Natchez District beginning in 1787 and later, in 1797, became Governor-General of Spanish Louisiana and West Florida as the successor of the Baron de Carondelet. Interestingly, Gayoso was married to two daughters of Dr. Flower's New Richmond partner Stephen Watts. First, in 1792 he married 19-year-old Elizabeth Watts, who died only three months after the marriage. Then Gayoso married her younger sister. Born in 1775 at Belmont on the Mississippi, Margaret Cyrilla Watts married the governor in 1796 and had one child before her husband died in office in 1799 at the age of 48.

By the 1790s Dr. Samuel Flower had moved with his wife to what is now West Feliciana on a series of Spanish land grants, now Butler Greenwood Plantation property. It is probable that he built the very first family house on a hill overlooking Bayou Sara and the agricultural fields. No one knows what that first house looked like, but it was surely in a beautiful and practical setting.

When Irish-born traveler Fortescue Cuming visited the area in 1809 while writing his travelogue *Sketches of a Tour to the Western Country,* he described the country along Bayou Sara to be "esteemed as the finest soil, the best cultivated, and inhabited by the most wealthy settlers, of any part of the Mississippi Territory or West Florida...on the whole a charming country." He visited Dr. Flower's home, where he received "the most pleasing attention," leading him to comment that being a stranger in the area "seems to be a general passport to hospitality."

The cultivated fields, planted first with indigo, then cotton and sugar cane, encompassed the flat land along Bayou Sara, enriched by creek overflow each spring as the flooding Mississippi River backed up into the bayou, which is both tributary and distributary to the larger river. The original brick-walled family cemetery is still on the hilltop, and only members of the first generation remain buried there. There are no signs of the house, which must have stood nearby, and after Grace Episcopal Church was established in 1827, succeeding generations were laid to rest in the cemetery surrounding the church (some were moved there after burial at home).

This peaceful cemetery at Grace Church is shaded by live oaks planted in the 1850s by faithful parishioner Harriett Flower Mathews, Dr. Flower's daughter, and among the earliest burials recorded was a small child whose cause of death was listed as "flung from buggy," no doubt a frequent occurrence in the days of runaway horses and wagons bouncing along rude, rutted roadways. On the first vestry were Judge Thomas Butler, Henry Flower and William Flower.

A letter written by Samuel Flower's great-granddaughter Sallie Mathews Ventress in 1932 says he came from "Reading or Redding, Pennsylvania", married in 1777, and journeyed for two years "to find a well-watered situation," finally settling in what is now West Feliciana Parish of Louisiana and establishing Greenwood Plantation. The first house was described as being about 2 miles from the present house seat on the plantation. The letter continues, "Their home was in a most beautiful situation overlooking the Bayou Sara Creek and the home of Don LeJeune and Madame Lejeune; my great-grandfather bought the lands of Don LeJeune and they are now part of Greenwood. My titles to this property are all in Spanish and I can't read one of them. They had their home and burying grounds there and that is one reason we have always clung to this old home; they are resting in the graveyard here." There are still ancient trees called the LeJeune Oaks close to the road that fords Bayou Sara creek, where the LeJeunes operated a little inn or tavern.

The children of Dr. Samuel Flower (1751 or 1754-1813) and Mary Carpenter Flower (1760-1812) were: Henry (1780-1780); Henry (1781-1840) whose daughter Maria married Andrew Collins, father-in-law of Grace Church rector Rev. Daniel Lewis who served about 1840-1868 (this may explain the Collins child's grave in the Mathews plot at Grace Church as Harriett Flower Mathews was godmother to a couple of the Reverend and Mrs. Harriet Lewis' children); William (1783-); Eliza (1785-); James (1787-) who married Lucy Griffiths and then Sara (Sally) Mulholland, whose son Charles Henry Flower married Clara Sprigg and had a son Charles Mulholland Flower; Samuel (1789-); Richard (1789-) who married Lucy Griffin (or did she marry brother James?) and had a son Richard who married Minerva Ann Scott, daughter of Judge Thomas W. Scott of Oakland near Gurley in East Feliciana Parish;

Harriett (1793-1873); Mathilda (1799-) who married Joseph Finley then Moses Lyon Meeker; Maria; Ames (1800-1808); Annie (1801-); and Julia (1803-1809). Cousinly congeniality had its amusing limits; one letter from Sallie Mathews Ventress, Dr. Flower's great-granddaughter who rarely minced words, said, "I have always heard Cousin Charles was a hard drinker and Cousin Clara a good spender. If I am telling too much, just do as Cousin Willie Fort used to say, 'Turn a blind ear and a deaf eye.'"

Dr. Samuel Flower's will was finalized July 9th, 1816, and left the homeplace to daughter Harriett. The will said, *"1st Harriett Mathews for herself, and by consent and jointly with George Mathews her husband, takes and receives of the effects of the estate, to wit, one plantation, the residence of the family at the time of, and subsequent to the demise of the said Samuel Flower, containing 800 arpents of land more or less, fronting on the Bayou Sarah... Appraised to and taken by the said Harriett Mathews for the sum of $12,500. Also one mulatto woman named Clia? of the age of seventeen years or thereabouts and her male child named Jack about 16 months appraised and taken at the sum of $800. Making together the sum of $13,300 which sum is acknowledged by the said Harriett Mathews, acting by the consent of and jointly with her husband as aforesaid, to have been received by them from the estate and to account to the heirs or their attornees for the same."*

Son James, who served as a lieutenant in the Bayou Sara Horse troop in the Battle of New Orleans along with Richard Carpenter's son James, received slaves and 800 arpents that had been granted to his father in 1797 between Thompson Creek and Alexander Creek called the Flower Place behind The Cottage Plantation; he married Sallie Mulholland Flower and they lived in her nice big Victorian house at the main intersection in St. Francisville where Parker Park is located, later called "Stocking Villa" for subsequent owner Dr. Stocking, a dentist whose daughter turned it into a hotel-type boarding house (Sally Mathews Ventress in a letter said, "She calls the place in compliment to her father Stocking Villa, and it don't look Silk Stocking, either"). Samuel Flower's daughter Maria Dalton received slaves; daughter Mathilda Finley received 600 arpents "having been granted to Mary Carpenter" on the south side of Alexander's Creek plus slaves; daughter Eliza Faulkner received slaves and property; son Henry had already received 400 arpents on Alexander's Creek; son David Flower 900 arpents on Coles Creek in the Mississippi Territory, and William land on the lower side of Bayou Manchac 9 miles from the river.

And concluding his will, dated January 10, 1814, Bayou Sara, State of Louisiana, Parish Feliciana (prior to division into East and West Feliciana), Dr. Flower "recommends to his family and executors that they cultivate and continue that harmony and fraternal affection which has heretofore existed between them and which has been a source of much satisfaction and comfort to me in my declining years and by all means avoid, as much as possible, that strife and contention which, in most cases, when once begun knows no end."

Had they only listened!

THE SECOND GENERATION

Harriett Flower and her husband Judge George Mathews

The children of Dr. Samuel Flower and his wife Mary Carpenter:

Henry (1780-1780), Henry (1781-1840), William (1783-), Eliza (1785-), James (1787-), Samuel (1789-), Richard (1789-1813), Harriett (1793-1873), Mathilda (1799-), Maria, Ames (1800-1808), Annie (1801-), and Julia (1803-1809).

HARRIETT FLOWER, who inherited the home place, was said, in one recent account, to have "provided a prototype of the women who followed in the family---independent, resourceful, successful, born of and bound to the land," and indeed the women of the family were generally long lived and, as widows, managed the plantation and everybody on it.

She married Judge George Mathews (1774-1836), well known to her father, Dr. Samuel Flower, as they had been brothers-in-law. The judge was first married to the half-sister of Samuel Flower's wife Mary Carpenter, and when she died an untimely death not long after giving birth to their only child, he married her young niece Harriett.

Judge Mathews' grandfather, John Mathews, had come to America during the Scotch-Irish immigration of the 1700s, married Ann Archer and had 11 children, among them Sampson, George, Archer and William. Samson and George were high-ranking officers in the Continental Army during the Revolutionary War.

Judge Mathews was the son of General George Mathews (1739-1812), who was born in Amherst County, Virginia, and died in Augusta, Georgia. He fought in the Indian Wars beginning at the age of 13, as a colonel commanded the 9th Virginia Regiment at the outbreak of the Revolutionary War, and led the troops into the fray at the Battle of Brandywine pitting George Washington's troops against Sir William Howe's British army (1777). He was severely wounded in a battle consisting mostly of hand-to-hand bayonet combat, was bayoneted as many as nine times, and was credited with saving American forces from being routed. He was later captured during the Battle of Germantown and confined first at Philadelphia and then on a prison ship anchored in New York harbor until 1781. Archival correspondence exists between General Mathews and Thomas Jefferson, who wrote to him in October 1779, "I beg you to be assured there is nothing consistent with the honour of your country which we shall not at all times be ready to do for the relief of yourself and companions in captivity. We know that ardent spirit and hatred for tyranny which brought you into your present situation will enable you to bear up against it with the firmness which has distinguished you as a solider..."

Upon his release, he rejoined the fray with General Nathaniel Green in South Carolina and Georgia. Having sensed fresh opportunity while serving with Green, he liquidated his Virginia property and in 1785 acquired land in Georgia, both through purchase and through land grants made for his Revolutionary War service. There he and his wife raised their eight children. He represented Georgia in the 1st Continental Congress (1789-1791), and was elected Governor of Georgia twice, 1787 and 1793-96. His involvement in the 25 million-acre Yazoo River controversy, along with Wade Hampton of South Carolina, soured his political fortunes and he left the state of Georgia, but later was still being considered for the governorship of the new Mississippi Territory.

During the international political wrangling over just where the eastern boundary of the 1803 Louisiana Purchase might be, St. Francisville was serving as the capital of the independent Republic of West Florida in the fall of 1810 after the rebellion that expelled the Spanish from what would become Louisiana's Florida Parishes, the toe of the boot-shaped state, in order to join the United States. Mathews, as a brigadier general, was sent by President Madison to Mobile and St. Augustine. There he was tasked with keeping an eye on the situation and maybe even fomenting a coordinated rebellion in hopes of annexing to the United States all of East Florida as well. This proved less successful than the West Florida Rebellion. Many controversies swirled around his fascinating political career, and he died on his journey to Washington to protect his honor regarding the various imbroglios of the Floridas.

George senior's first wife was Ann Paul, and after her death, late in life he married Mary Fairchild Lewis Carpenter, the widow of Daniel Lewis and then Richard Carpenter, in 1804 in Natchez; she was the stepmother of Mary Carpenter, wife of Dr. Samuel Flower (the parents of his son Judge George Mathews' wife Harriett), and she was also the mother of Judge Mathews' first wife Sarah Carpenter.

Colonel Thomas Rodney, member of the Continental Congress and Judge of the US Court for the Territory of Mississippi, recorded an account of a visit with old General George Mathews (father of the judge) in which he says the general served in the Indian warfare in Virginia, was colonel of the 9th Virginia Regiment in the Revolutionary War, was wounded and taken prisoner at Germantown in 1777 and exchanged in 1781 to join General Greene's army in the south as colonel of the 3rd (12th?) Virginia Regiment. He removed to Georgia in 1785, was representative to the first Congress held under the Constitution of the United States, served as governor of Georgia 1793-1796, was in Natchez to visit his son whom President Jefferson had appointed a judge on one of the US Courts of the Territory in 1805, "and was married last summer to the widow Carpenter by Myself...The General is a Ruff brave old Soldier and is in many respects Respectable...nor does he lack Strong Talants (sic) but all his Opportunities have not polished them much."

His son, Judge George Mathews, was born in Staunton, Virginia, in 1774, was educated at Liberty Hall in Lexington, Virginia, and died in Bayou Sara, Louisiana, at his home, Greenwood Plantation now known as Butler Greenwood Plantation, in 1836. He studied law with his brother John in Augusta, Georgia, and was admitted to the Georgia bar in 1799. He was appointed by President Thomas Jefferson to serve as first federal judge of the Superior Court of the Mississippi Territory in 1805, and then was appointed judge of the Territorial Court for Louisiana 1806-1813. Corresponding in 1806 with Jefferson upon notification of his appointment as one of the judges for the Territory of Orleans, Judge Mathews expressed pleasant surprise at the appointment and said, "I accept the appointment and take the liberty of tendering you my sincere thanks, for the confidence reposed in me, evidenced by a nomination to so important a judicial Office. Confident, that a determined resolution to do right, is the surest means of effecting it, the diffidence which I feel in my adequacy to a reputable performance of the duties, attached to a situation so responsible is considerably lessened..." As a territorial judge he "rode circuit" on horseback, covering the area from Natchez to Natchitoches, Alexandria, Opelousas and St. Francisville.

In 1808 Judge Mathews again wrote to Thomas Jefferson to suggest that Seth Lewis be considered for the vacancy on the Bench of the Superior Court of the Orleans Territory. Lewis, of the Mississippi Territory, was said to be learned in the Law, fluent in French and Spanish, incorruptible, honest, capable and a friend of the Constitution and government of the United States (not to mention that Seth Lewis was the son of the first marriage of Mary Fairchild Lewis Carpenter Mathews whose marriage to the father of Judge Mathews would make the two stepbrothers, plus the Judge's first wife was Seth's half-sister).

Edwin Adams Davis listed Mathews among several noted antebellum lawyers and characterized him as "short, rotund and placid, with good humor and good taste."

After Louisiana became a state, Judge George Mathews was appointed in March of 1813 by Governor William C.C. Claiborne to serve as one of three judges on the first Louisiana Supreme Court; in July of 1813 he became the Chief Justice, presiding over the court in that capacity until his death. His decisions did much to form a permanent system of jurisprudence in Louisiana, and he played an important role in combining the common law tradition with the civil law tradition as Louisiana's legal institutions were Americanized.

Volume X of the Louisiana Supreme Court records, printed 1837, reported the death of Judge George Mathews at his residence near Bayou Sara the 14th of November 1836, "after presiding in the Supreme Court of Louisiana 23 years and in the Territorial Court 7. Judge Mathews' loss is severely felt, and deeply deplored by the people of Louisiana. He was an able jurist, an upright judge, a man of spotless integrity, over whom the good and excellent qualities of our nature constantly predominated. He possessed a sound judgment, and a rare combination of sagacity of intellect, with a powerful instinct of natural justice and equity. Seldom equaled, and never, perhaps, surpassed."

He had been married to Harriet's aunt Sarah Carpenter (daughter of Richard Carpenter), by whom he had a daughter Ann Paul Mathews (1809-1863). Ann married Major William Henry Chase (1798-1870), US Military Academy graduate and engineer corps, designer of the forts at Mobile and Pensacola. As senior engineer of the Gulf frontier for the US Army Corps of Engineers, he built Forts Pickens, McRee, Barrancas and an advanced redoubt not finished. Appointed Superintendent of the US Military Academy, he later resigned from the army, became president of the Alabama and Florida Railroad, then joined the Confederacy and was active in the seizure of Pensacola navy-yard.

At the outbreak of the Civil War, he was a colonel in charge of the state militia at Pensacola. He demanded the surrender of Fort Pickens from US Army Lt. Adam Slemmer, but was so emotional at the thought of fighting against the fort he had built that he stamped his foot and couldn't read the words he had prepared, so he handed his speech to a subordinate to read; Slemmer turned down the ultimatum and Fort Pickens remained in Union hands throughout the war. The Chase family from which he descended got its start in this country in New Hampshire with a group of settlers who received a grant of land in 1640.

Chase and his wife Ann Paul Mathews spent much of their married life living in Pensacola, and they had one daughter. They also lived at Chaseland in Rapides Parish, where Major Chase drew the plans for Trinity Episcopal Church in Cheneyville. Ann Paul Mathews had been raised by Harriett Flower and her husband Judge George Mathews (father of Ann) after the early death of her mother Sarah Carpenter Mathews, first wife of Judge George Mathews and the aunt of Harriett. Sarah died at age 23 in 1811 at Bayou Boeuf, Parish of Rapides. Her newspaper obituary read, "In the character of this excellent lady were united all those endearing and domestic qualities which sweeten life and render it desirable. Long, very long will her untimely departure from this scene of existence draw the sigh of sorrow from the bosoms of those relatives and friends who are yet left to the toil of life."

Harriett Flower Mathews (1793-1873), of Butler Greenwood Plantation, long outlived her husband. Through all her years of widowhood, she managed to run four plantations and with her son was cited as being among the top sugar planters in the state prior to the Civil War. She managed properties in Lafourche Parish (Georgia Plantation in the community of Mathews, near Raceland), West Feliciana Parish (Greenwood Plantation, now called Butler Greenwood), and Rapides Parish (Chaseland and Coco Bend). She was a remarkably strong woman who held onto her properties during and after the Civil War, travelling to New Orleans by steamboat during the hostilities to check with her cotton factor, her brother William Flower who as family commission merchant was responsible for the sale of the cotton and sugar crops, and ruling the plantations with an iron fist until her death. She not only outlived her husband, but also all of her children, and she was a plantation mistress who kept careful records of her finances and her properties, including large numbers of slaves whose names, ages, medical needs and clothing sizes she knew, as evidenced by the lists of clothing she ordered the plantation seamstresses to make for them.

Harriett Flower and Judge George Mathews had two sons, George Mathews who died as a boy (1817-1824) and Charles Lewis Mathews (1824-1864) who was named for the Judge's brother. They most certainly lived in the second house on the plantation, located away from the Bayou Sara fields and closer to the road leading to Natchez and then Up East along the Natchez Trace. Had this house been built by Harriett's father Dr. Flower before his death? Perhaps. It is certainly typical of the early houses in the area, raised rambling cottage-style homes built for the climate, with broad galleries to shade the interior, no central hall so that every room opens to the outside, high ceilings and floor-to-ceiling windows or French doors. Practical but unpretentious. In one old article from the Baton Rouge newspaper, probably from the mid-1900s, former garden editor Al Alleman describes a visit with resident family members. "The house originally was built in 1778, but it burned and was rebuilt in a different location on the property in 1800. In 1820 it was enlarged and has remained substantially the same to this day." The Butler Greenwood house was considered significant enough to be listed on the National Register of Historic Places in 1979, not only because of its association with important family members but also for its architecture and landscapes, the house design showing early and mid-19th-century influences and the landscape combining English and French features.

It is more likely that the enlargements, including a two-story wing addition, were done in the 1850s when the family had the most money, plus had multi-generational occupancy and needed extra space; after Judge Mathews died, his widow Harriett, son Charles Lewis Mathews and his wife Penelope Stewart, all their children, an Irish gardener and an Austrian music teacher lived in the house. Also, Harriett had raised Judge Mathews' daughter Ann by his first wife who died shortly after the child's birth, and she was in and out of residence at Greenwood even in adulthood and often travelled with the family. The 1850's also were the period when Harriett embellished the original simple English-style cottage with fancier gallery rail across the front, Victorian trim (later removed), and formalized the parlor into one of the most important interiors extant in the state.

The house is surrounded by extensive groves of live oaks and formal gardens begun by Harriett Mathews in the 1840s, judging from preserved orders of garden implements and flower seed, tools, pots and plants. To the north of the house are formal parterre gardens, reminiscent of geometric landscapes in 16th and 17th-century French gardens, and recorded in the first Historic American Building Survey in Louisiana in 1941, the only state garden recorded and one of less than thirty in the nation. Along the entrance drive is a less formal sunken garden.

In contrast to the gardens, the frontal landscape contains live oaks planted in a naturalized, free-flowing manner typical of 18th-century English design, more in harmony with nature than the formalized oak allees. It is this house, now called Butler Greenwood Plantation, which is still occupied by family descendants.

THE THIRD GENERATION

Charles Lewis Mathews and his wife Penelope Stewart

The children of Harriett Flower Mathews and Judge George Mathews: George (1817-1824) and Charles Lewis (1824-1864)

Charles Lewis Mathews, handsome son of Harriett Flower and Judge George Mathews, was born the year of his older brother's death as a small boy. He attended Trinity College in Hartford, Connecticut.

While he was there, his mother visited him and purchased from nurseries in the Northeast camellia plants for the extensive formal gardens being established at Greenwood, probably in the early 1840s. Still remaining in the gardens are boxwood hedges in a maze, enormous magnolia fuscata, more than 150 camellias and sasanquas grown to tree size, huge sweet olive, hundreds of live oaks, several gingko trees, eleagenous, tons of azaleas, and an unusual peacock running moss that is blue-green in summer and pink-bronze in fall. The parterre gardens were studied and mapped in the 1930s-40s Historic American Building Survey studies of significant architecture and landscapes across the country, and these blueprints are preserved in the National Archives in Washington, D.C., along with drawings of the stepped-façade outside kitchen, certainly one of the oldest structures in the parish. Garden editor Al Alleman called the gardens, in their heyday requiring 30 gardeners, among the finest in the state.

In 1848 Charles Lewis Mathews married the beautiful dark-haired Penelope Stewart (1828-1897) of Holly Grove Plantation in Centerville, MS. Together they had a number of children, although as a boy in 1836, the year of his father's death, he had shot himself in the right arm climbing through a fence with a shotgun while hunting and was not able to participate in the Civil War other than in a supply and support capacity. Their offspring were Harriett (1856-1922), George (1849-1859), Charles Stewart (1858-1918/20), Sallie (1859-1934), George (1860-1907), William Fort (1862-1881), and Annie Chase (1864-1864).

The Mathews family lived at Butler Greenwood Plantation and raised first indigo, then cotton, sugarcane and corn, shipping the crops from their own dock on Bayou Sara and extending their landholdings to include a productive sugar plantation in Lafourche Parish that, according to Lewis Gray's figures, placed them among the top 9% of sugar planters in the state in the 1850's. After the death of Judge Mathews in 1836, his widow continued to run the plantations with help from her son Charles, who as a 19-year-old was sent to Havana, Cuba, in 1843 to learn all he could about sugar planting. When he was 21, he took over management of the two plantations in Rapides Parish.

In 1830 Judge Mathews headed a household consisting of ten whites and 35 slaves. By the census of 1860, both Harriett and her son list their occupations as "planter," their household including Charles' wife Penelope Stewart, their children, an Austrian music teacher and an Irish gardener, with 96 slaves living in 18 dwellings, and their personal estate valued at $260,000. In that year the 1400 acres of Butler Greenwood Plantation produced 130 bales of cotton (400-pound bales), 2000 bushels of corn, 175 hogsheads of sugar (one hogshead weighed 1,000 pounds) and more than 10,000 gallons of molasses. Their other plantations covered nearly 10,000 acres worked by some 400 slaves, and it was not uncommon for the labor force to be moved from one plantation to another as needed. These other plantations were equally productive in 1860. After the Civil War, though, the labor force had fallen to a field gang of only 27 freedmen working for monthly wages on the home place, and many of them were former slaves who wished to stay on the plantation.

The census of 1870 showed 77-year-old Harriett as head of household, her real estate valued at only $5,000 and personal estate $2,500; the freedmen were paid $12-$15 a month for first-rate hands, second-rate (usually women) $6-$10 a month. In 1866 the written "Rules and Regulations for the Plantation known as Greenwood" stipulated forbidden actions and punishments: causing trouble, inciting insurrection, taking livestock without permission, improper care of animals. Workmen were required to retire to their quarters after work "and stay away from the corn crib," and they were fined for smoking a pipe or cigar within 500 feet of the barn or stable. Fines were placed in a pool which was divided "among the good and faithful hands" at year's end.

Before the hard times of the Civil War, antebellum records show Charles purchasing pricey hunting dogs and indulging himself with luxury items like two buggies imported from New York, a gold hunting watch, and fine gentleman's clothing from Cordville and LaCroix, earning a rebuke from his frugal mother. But this was in 1845, and he was, after all, courting; he would marry the lovely Penelope Stewart in 1848. The family travelled extensively, having oil portraits done of the adults and hand-tinted early photographs made of two of their small daughters, Sallie and Harriett, in New York in 1860, probably their last trip north. When Charles died in 1864, his widow Penelope continued helping his mother Harriett until her death.

Penelope Jones Stewart's father was Tignal Jones Stewart (1800-1855) who in 1825 had married Sallie Anne Randolph (1809-1892). Penelope's paternal grandparents were Duncan Stewart, lieutenant governor of Mississippi, and Penelope Jones Stewart (1779-1843), the daughter of Colonel Tignal Jones of North Carolina who was governor of Tennessee; they had married in 1798 and in 1811 moved to Mississippi where they built Holly Grove Plantation near Centerville. Grandparents on Penelope's maternal side were Sallie Cocke and her husband Judge Peter Randolph of Virginia, who moved to Mississippi to settle new land claims and in 1822 was appointed by President Monroe as Judge of the Court of Error and Appeals in Mississippi. Two of Duncan Stewart's sons married sisters from the Randolph family (Nottoway Plantation builder John Hampton Randolph was their brother), and their children married into West Feliciana families including the Forts of Catalpa Plantation and of course the Mathews of Butler Greenwood.

The Stewart line in America begins with William Stewart, who came to North Carolina from Scotland in 1739 with a company of immigrants consisting of his elder brother Patrick, six Argyleshire gentlemen and "about 300 common people." William's second wife bore him 8 children, including Duncan who married Penelope Jones and his twin brother James; these two are buried at Holly Grove. Duncan served as state representative and senator in North Carolina and then also in Tennessee, coming to the Mississippi Territory in 1809/11. There he served as surveyor general of the territory and a legislator and, after statehood, first lieutenant governor of Mississippi.

The Stewart family originated in Brittany, and Robert II was king of Scotland 1371-1390, founder of the Stewart dynasty that ruled Scotland and later England as well. They descended from a long line of kings and earls, the Royal Stewarts, beginning with King Duncan whose son Malcolm III became king of Scotland in 1054; through Malcolm's wife, the children were lineal descendants of Alfred the Great, and one married King Henry I of England. A few generations down, a daughter married Robert Bruce of Norman descent, and generations were kings of Scotland and Ireland until we get to Robert The Bruce (1274-1329), the great champion of Scottish independence.

So we have the Mathews connection being bayoneted nine times and living to fight again, then the Stewart family of mighty warriors including Robert The Bruce. Enough to give pacifistic Quaker ancestors nightmares; and then just wait for the militaristic Butlers to marry into the family!

The Fourth Generation

Sallie Mathews and her husband James Alexander Ventress

The children of Charles Lewis Mathews and Penelope Stewart Mathews: Harriett (1856-1922), George (1849-1859), Charles Stewart (1858-1918/20), Sallie (1859-1934), George (1860-1907), William Fort (1862-1881), Annie Chase (1864-1864)

Charles Lewis Mathews and his wife Penelope Stewart had seven children. Harriett Mathews (1856-1922) in 1875 married Samuel McCutcheon Lawrason (1852-1924). George Mathews (1849-1859) died as a small boy. Charles Stewart Mathews (1858-1918/20) supervised the family properties in Lafourche Parish in South Louisiana and married late in life to a widow with a daughter who occasioned a legal fight over property ownership and occasioned the bitter wording of his sister Sallie's will. Sallie Mathews (1859-1934), called Auntie, married late in life to James Alexander Ventress, Jr. (1853-1911) of Woodville. George Mathews was born in 1860 and died in 1907. William Fort Mathews (1862-1881) was called Fortie and died young (note the middle name Fort, since his mother Penelope Stewart was sister of Willie Fort of Catalpa's wife Sallie). Little Annie Chase Mathews was born and died in 1864 and her name lives on in the eighth generation in the house.

It would be Sallie Mathews who stayed at home to take care of her grandmother and mother as they aged. In 1897, more than 30 years after her husband's death, Penelope Mathews died at Greenwood. Sallie received this consoling note from her brother Charles: "I trust this will find you reconciled to our loss and certainly you have nothing to reproach yourself for, as your life has been given to Mother's care and welfare. If the dead could have communication with the living you would only hear blessings."

So she did not marry until late in life. Her husband James Alexander Ventress, Jr., (1853-1911) was also elderly. They had no children, but apparently enjoyed an active life, travelling to Saratoga for the season with his famous trotting horses and to other Victorian wateringholes. Their woodpile for the fireplaces at Greenwood (one in every room) was said to stretch all the way across the back yard and then back again.

He was the son of a moneyed Mississippi planter with ties to the Stewart family; Lovick Ventress had come down from Tennessee to Mississippi in 1809 with his brother-in-law Duncan Stewart and wife Penelope. Lovick's son James Alexander Ventress, Sr., was one of Wilkinson County, Mississippi's richest and most prominent planters. He was also a state legislator, civic leader, owner of thousands of acres in Mississippi and Louisiana, and one of the founders of the University of Mississippi.

When Sallie Mathews Ventress died, having carried on the family tradition of surviving widows by outliving her husband by several decades, she was also considered quite wealthy, especially for the midst of the Great Depression. It was her will that infamously tried to disinherit the heir of her brother, unsuccessfully and unnecessarily. Her 1934 succession lists 1248.79 acres of Greenwood, 372.9 acres of Maynard tract attached to the north end of Greenwood, 550 acres in Cat Island, plus over $105,000 worth of stock, farm tools, livestock, silver, and household furniture considerably undervalued (the priceless 12-piece parlor set was valued at $140, the 1855 rosewood French Pleyel concert grand piano valued at $5, etc.) The will stipulates "no bastard named xxxxx shall inherit one penny," because she questioned the relationship of the child to her brother Charles; he managed the family sugar properties in Raceland called Georgia Plantation and apparently took up as an old man with his nurse, mother of the child. As an adult, this child was a lovely lady who had very cordial relations with subsequent generations of Mathews descendants, but not with the opinionated Auntie.

When she died childless, she left the Greenwood property to her sister Harriett's daughter, Annie Mathews Lawrason Butler.

Harriett Mathews married Judge Samuel McCutcheon Lawrason. They lived at Clover Hill Plantation (now Girl Scout Camp Marydale), and they had seven children: Zelia McCutcheon Lawrason was born in 1876 and died in 1916. Annie Mathews Lawrason was born in 1878 and died in 1962, attended Silliman Institute in Clinton and was a great horticulturist who during the Depression operated a plant nursery at Greenwood, which she inherited from her aunt Sallie Mathews Ventress; she married Edward Butler (1871-1948) of The Cottage Plantation, and they lived there until the death of Auntie, when they moved to Greenwood. Charles Lawrason was born in 1882 and died in 1955. Helen Stewart Lawrason (1884-1963) married Douglas Kilpatrick (grandparents of Rob and Laurie Fisher). Thomas Butler Lawrason (1887-1960) married Alice Golsan and their children were Florence, Butler and JoAnne. George Carson Lawrason married Blanche Powell (1896-1948) and had one son, George. Samuel Lawrason died at 6 months. Levering Lawrason was born in 1893 and moved to California, where he married and had children. And Margarett Lawrason, who was born in 1888, never married, spent some years in New Orleans and then lived with her sister Annie at Greenwood, died in 1977 and after Annie's death she lived with her nephew Murrell Butler.

Judge Samuel McCutcheon Lawrason, after announcing his (unsuccessful) candidacy for state lieutenant governor, was said in the St. Francisville *True Democrat* of June 1, 1907, to have "a judicial, deliberative mind, calm and dispassionate, slow to wrath and excitement and of great patience, with a well-trained, highly cultured mind, the courtly manner of the thorough gentleman, and a noble character without fear and without reproach."

His father George Carson Lawrason (1816-1875) had married Zelia Henderson McCutcheon around 1850. He was Collector of the Port of New Orleans and was imprisoned on Ship Island for two years after the city fell to northern forces during the Civil War. Zelia took her two small sons to Barcelona, Spain, where she died in 1864. The boys were educated in European schools, including in France and on the Isle of Jersey, until their father was able to return them to the states. Samuel went to Washington & Lee University and Virginia Military Institute (class of 1872), and family lore mentions his participation in Robert E. Lee's funeral in 1870 while a student in Lexington. There is at Greenwood a fine sword with silver eagle's head and ivory embellishments. He later graduated from law school at Tulane University in New Orleans.

His grandparents on one side, Thomas Lawrason (1780-1819) who in 1808 married Elizabeth Carson (1792-1851), lived in Alexandria, Virginia. Their home is now called the Lafayette House, as it was visited by General Lafayette and also supposedly by Robert E. Lee. Family stories say this friendship meant that, as a student in Lexington while General Lee was teaching at what was then Washington College, Samuel was often invited to Sunday supper with the Lee family. Grandmother Elizabeth came to Louisiana from Virginia to live with her son and family, died in 1851 and was buried in the McCutcheon family graveyard at Ormond Plantation; when the Mississippi River overflowed and inundated the cemetery, her body was swept away. Judge Samuel McCutcheon Lawrason's grandparents on the other side were Samuel McCutcheon and Rebecca Butler, daughter of Colonel William Butler and his wife Jane Carmichael; Rebecca owned Ormond Plantation with her brother Richard Butler.

After the death of his wife Zelia Henderson McCutcheon, Judge Lawrason's father George Carson Lawrason married Sarah Pirrie Smith, widow of James Stirling and daughter of Jedidiah Smith and Mary Ann Gray (daughter of Ruffin Gray of Oakley Plantation and step daughter of James Pirrie, half-sister of Eliza Pirrie, Audubon's pupil). Mary Ann Gray had first married Jedidiah Smith, and when he died, she married Dr. Ira Smith of Troy Plantation and Smithfield.

Samuel McCutcheon Lawrason returned to New Orleans after college, read law, and married Harriett Mathews in 1875. They lived at Clover Hill Plantation in her home parish, later building the stately townhouse called Hillcroft in St. Francisville on Royal St. so that the judge could be nearer his law office and the parish courthouse. They had nine children.

He was a parish judge, state senator, vice-president of Louisiana's controversial Constitutional Convention of 1898, president of Louisiana Bankers Association in 1905, and for many years he served on the parish school board and on the State Board of Education.

He also served on LSU's Board of Supervisors for over 30 years, from 1886 when he became a Supervisor of LSU to the date of his death, and a Faculty Resolution paid this tribute to him: *"The death of Judge Samuel McCutcheon Lawrason at his home in St. Francisville on November 7, 1924, has spread profound sorrow among the members of the University Faculty who knew him personally and who valued his great services to the institution as a member of its governing board. From 1886 when he became a Supervisor of the University to the date of his death Judge Lawrason never missed a meeting of the Board of Supervisors until his last illness made attendance impossible. For most of the time during that long period he served as a member of the Executive Committee, and dedicated to the important duties he performed in both capacities the strong, symmetrical character, the rich experience, and the stimulating vision that commanded the admiration of all who knew him…By those of us who possessed the privilege of Judge Lawrason's friendship he will always be remembered as the southern gentleman par excellence, strong in the Christian's faith, charitable in his outlook upon the world, courteous and hospitable in his social relations, and admirable in his home life. Faith in our civilization is strengthened and sustained by the life of such a man. May the future bring to the services of the State others with the same ideals of civic righteousness."*

The New Orleans *Times-Picayune* obituary said, "For more than 50 years Judge Lawrason exemplified good citizenship of the finest and most useful type. Gaining distinction in his chosen profession, he devoted much study, and gave freely of his time and ability, to public affairs. His service on the bench and in the State Senate was only a fractional part of the service he rendered the state and its people during the half-century of his active life. He was an honored and influential figure in Louisiana's constitutional, educational and civic councils. His uprightness, honesty and independence of thought, and the sturdy courage which always supported his convictions, made him a force to be reckoned with in the political life of the state."

The local *True Democrat* article at the time of his death mourned his passing while excusing his failure to be elected to high political office by saying, "Judge Lawrason was a type of man who is seldom successful in the higher branches of politics. His integrity was unswerving, and he would not stoop to the wiles of the politician in an effort to secure votes. Twice he was a candidate for State office, each time securing a large popular vote, and failing of election only because leaders in the game of politics knew that he was irreproachable and that he would not swerve from the path of duty to that of expediency… In the passing of Judge Lawrason West Feliciana loses the most outstanding figure of his generation—a man whose life served as example and inspiration to others, and whose passing arouses regret in the hearts of all who knew him." In reporting on his funeral, the *True Democrat* issue of November 25, 1923, said, "He was generous without show and charitable without publicity, being ever ready to use his talents, time and money on behalf of any worthy cause or for the softening of sorrow in any form. His commanding presence and courtly manners were an inspiration to all with whom he came in contact."

THE FIFTH GENERATION

Annie Mathews Lawrason and her husband Edward G. Butler

Since Sallie Mathews Ventress died childless, she left Greenwood to her sister Harriett's daughter.

The children of Harriett Mathews Lawrason and Judge Samuel McCutcheon Lawrason: Zelia McCutcheon (1876-1916), Annie Mathews (1878-1962), Charles (1882-1955), Helen Stewart (1884-1963), Thomas Butler (1887-1960), George Carson (1879-1941), Samuel (died 6 mos.), Levering (1893-), and Margarett (1888-1977).

Judge Samuel McCutcheon Lawrason and his wife Harriett Mathews Lawrason had a daughter Annie Mathews Lawrason, who inherited the Greenwood Plantation property and house from her mother's sister Sallie Mathews Ventress, who died without issue. After living at her husband's family home, The Cottage Plantation, for 30-something years, the couple moved into the Greenwood house in the 1930s.

Annie Mathews Lawrason, my grandmother, was a great horticulturist who operated a plant nursery during the Depression to try to make ends meet. She was a poet and was exceptionally well read (there are thousands of books on every subject in the library at Greenwood); her husband was an expert ornithologist and planter. She outlived him by many years but managed to keep the place together, raising beef cattle and horses. With the help of her ethereal maiden sister Margarett (called Mock) and a number of gardeners, she maintained the extensive formal gardens where there was, as author James Lee Burke so beautifully said, sunlight sifting like spiritual grace through oak limbs and Spanish moss.

Mock lived in the back bedroom on the second floor of the enormous high-ceilinged wing added to the north side of the main house in the 1850s, while my grandmother lived as far on the other side of the house as possible, in the master bedroom with floor-to-ceiling windows opening onto the broad front gallery. White-haired Mock puttered around in the garden wearing a sundress with sturdy heels with socks and usually a broad-brimmed sun hat. She loved cats; one mischievous young cousin, male of course, tested the theory of cats' abilities to land on their feet by throwing one out of Mock's upstairs window. It lived up to its reputation.

My grandmother was blessed to have the help of devoted and much loved servants (Celie Williams the cook, Gertrude Veal the housekeeper, Hattie Johnson the laundress, Wallace Williams the yardman/chauffeur who was husband to Harriett Veal, Nolan Veal and Duncan Veal and Lawrence called Gator who looked after the livestock) who were mostly descendants of Jones Veal, one of the enslaved whose family stayed on the place for generations, sharecropped and then worked for wages, had their own houses and were well regarded by the family.

Celie did all the cooking in the outside kitchen, with Gertrude carrying dishes in on big trays to serve in the main house dining room, until my grandmother's death in 1962. Gertrude lived long enough to babysit the eighth generation of this family, a tall big-boned woman with very erect posture who was said to have Indian blood in her background.

Huge multi-course Sunday dinners fed grown children and grandchildren, other relatives and friends, with the main dining table for adults and card tables set up for children. It was a wonder there was food enough for the multitudes, but there was an enormous vegetable garden and poultry yards full of chickens, ducks, turkeys, with fattening coops and brooders. The pond behind the house, ringed with native Louisiana iris, was for the Muscovy ducks, but there were lots of fish in it, too, and this was the original farm-to-table set-up. At some point even hogs and sheep were raised on the place.

Annie Mathews Lawrason Butler was born in 1878 and died in 1962; her husband Edward Gaillard Butler was seven years her senior and died in 1948, leaving her to manage the Greenwood Property alone for fourteen years. She did receive help from her four children, who were mostly grown when she inherited Greenwood, and she would give each of them part of the property; two of them built their own houses on it. There were three boys and one girl. Oldest son Edward Lawrason Butler, called Laurie, married Gwin Murrell of Tally Ho Plantation near White Castle, and they had two children, Edward Murrell Butler the nationally respected bird artist, and Patrick Lawrason Butler who married Lucie Ewing and had three daughters (Margaret called Meg, Louise called Weeze, and Adair). Next, the only daughter, elegant Harriett Mathews Butler, born in 1901 and died in 1973, married in 1934 noted New Orleans maritime attorney James Henry Bruns who was born in 1894. Uncle Henry, called by some neighbors Uncle Hungry for his propensity for showing up at mealtime, was a real character who retired from legal work and moved to the country with his prize English setter and his mother-in-law (leaving wife and daughter to New Orleans society); he had a fondness for working in his vegetable garden wearing nothing but a bandana and a jockstrap, much to the consternation of the ladies of the house, especially when the Episcopal minister's wife came calling. They had one daughter Virginia Cox Bruns (1935-) who married Samuel Marshall and their children are Anne, Frances and James. Next son was Charles Mathews Butler, born in 1910 and died in 1971, my father, who married Katharine Minor Pipes Butler (1922-1982) of Southdown Plantation in Terrebonne Parish, and their children were Anne Lawrason Butler (me) and Mary Minor Butler Hebert. Last child was Robert Ormond Butler (1919-), much decorated World War II veteran of the 82nd Airborne, who married Mary Minor Pipes Butler (1925-) sister of her husband's brother's wife Katharine, and their children are Virginia Pipes Butler who married Michael Healy and their children are Kate and Annie, and Robert Ormond Butler, Jr., who married Elizabeth Adkins and their children are Mary Minor, Elizabeth Anne, and Jeanne Cody.

Lest this sound too much like the interminable Biblical *begats*, the Butler family certainly enlivened the family tree, and the *begats* are necessary to show the million blood ties between all the different branches of the early plantation families here. There were, after all, only so many respectable pioneering families in the area in the early days, so it's no wonder that they socialized and intermarried.

The Butlers were proudly Irish in origin, one of three Norman families outstanding in the molding of Irish history in the centuries following the invasion of 1169, and no Irish family produced such a succession of able administrators, churchmen and soldiers. The family founder was Theobald FitzWalter I who came to Ireland in 1171 with Henry II. Theobald was appointed Chief Butler of Ireland to Henry II, a hereditary office giving its name to the family, with duties including attending the king at his coronation and presenting him his first cup of wine.

When James, the 7th Butler, married the granddaughter of King Edward I of England, he was created Earl of Ormond. This first Duke of Ormond held the office of Lord Lieutenant of Ireland and was buried at Westminster Abbey when he died. His grandson, the second Duke of Ormond, was chancellor of the University of Oxford in 1688 and commanded the armies under both William of Orange and Queen Anne. James Butler, 3rd Earl of Ormond, was Lord Justice of Ireland and purchased Kilkenny Castle, which the Ormonds made their chief seat and residence from the 1390s through the 1920s, and there he hosted King Richard II. His wife, Anne Butler, was the first Countess of Ormond to live at Kilkenny Castle.

The daughter of the 7th Earl married Sir William Boleyne, grandfather of Anne Boleyne, ill-fated second queen of King Henry VIII. With no direct Ormond heir, the Boleynes were made Earls of Ormond, and it was Anne's father Sir Thomas Boleyne, Butler on the distaff and Earl of Ormond, who was the King's brilliant ambassador abroad. When Henry VIII wanted to have the Pope sanction a dissolution of his marriage to his first queen Katherine of Aragon so he could marry Anne, he sent Sir Thomas to have an audience with the Pope, who discreetly advanced his foot to be kissed as was the custom. When the Earl ignored the proferred foot, the Pope pushed out his slipper rather more decisively, and the Earl's dog, thinking his master about to be attacked, bit the papal toe, widening the rift between Henry and Rome (this fascinating tidbit comes from the July 1967 issue of *Ireland of the Welcomes*, article entitled "The Butlers").

The 10th Earl of Ormond (1531-1614) was the son of James Butler, the 9th Earl, and his wife Lady Jane Fitzgerald, the daughter of the 10th Earl of Desmond. He was called Black Tom, not for having a dark complexion but for besting another Thomas called White Tom, Sir Thomas Wyatt, while quelling that Tom's rebellion against Queen Mary. Queen Elizabeth I, a fifth cousin once removed through her mother Anne Boleyn, was very close to him, perhaps suspiciously close; she made him a Knight of the Garter (rare honor for an Irishman) and was said to have toyed with the idea of marrying him. She called him her black husband, and in fact there were rumors of his being the father of her illegitimate son Piers (Pierce) Butler. Black Tom married three times, had three or four legitimate children and a dozen known illegitimate children, but favored Piers above all others in his will. He was said to have died in the bedroom of the Tudor castle he had built for Queen Elizabeth should she visit Ireland, with the Knight of the Garter insignia she'd given him around his neck.

It was in 1748 that Thomas Butler, born in 1720, came from County Wicklow, Ireland, to America. Marriage to Sara Jane Semple produced a dozen children, including sons called by George Washington the "Five Fighting Butlers" of the Revolutionary War. Several were mere teens at war's onset, but they fought valiantly on the American side, gaining high rank and that toast from George Washington, with whom they endured the harsh winter of 1777-8 at Valley Forge. Excuse the pacifist Quaker ancestor's shudder.

One of the five sons, Richard Butler, was a Major General and was designated to place the American flag on the British works after the surrender of Cornwallis at Yorktown. Just before his heroic death in the Battle of Miami against the Indians in 1791 he was placed second in command of the US Army. He was tomahawked in that battle and mortally wounded, scalped, and his heart was eaten by the redskins in tribute to his bravery; his brother Colonel Thomas Butler was shot through both legs but was saved by a third brother.

Another of the five sons, William, was a colonel. His son Colonel Richard Butler served with five cousins on the immediate staff of General Andrew Jackson at the Battle of New Orleans. In 1805 he purchased Ormond Plantation on the River Road, naming it for his Irish ancestors. He had four children but died of yellow fever on the Mississippi Gulf Coast at age 43, and his sister Rebecca (1809-1881) inherited Ormond Plantation. Rebecca, daughter of Colonel William Butler, married Philadelphia seaman/merchant Captain Samuel McCutcheon, and they had nine children. One of their sons, Samuel, married Adele Destrehan of Destrehan Plantation, while their daughter Zelia married George C. Lawrason, head of the Port of New Orleans when Civil War began. It was his son Judge Samuel McCutcheon Lawrason of Clover Hill Plantation and Hillcroft in St. Francisville who married Harriett Mathews of Butler Greenwood Plantation, whose daughter Annie Mathews Lawrason married Edward G. Butler of The Cottage Plantation in West Feliciana Parish, and their son Charles Mathews Butler married Katharine Minor Pipes of Southdown Plantation, and their daughter Anne Lawrason Butler (me) would be the seventh generation to live at Butler Greenwood.

One of the five sons, Percival, was an Adjutant General.

Another of the five sons, Edward, was also an Adjutant General. His son, Edward George Washington Butler

(1800-1888), was made the ward of General Andrew Jackson after the death of his father. Edward George Washington Butler's wife was Frances Parke Lewis, daughter of Eleanor Parke Custis (Martha Washington's granddaughter) and Lawrence Lewis (George Washington's nephew).

One of the five sons, Thomas, was born in 1748 in Dublin, Ireland, and rose to the rank of Colonel. He married Sara Jane Semple, born in 1764 in Pennsylvania, and moved to New Orleans after the Louisiana Purchase to serve as executive officer to the new American governor, W.C.C. Claiborne, who had instructions from President Jefferson to Americanize the French-speaking Louisianians as soon as possible. With four of his brothers, he had fought with such distinction in the American Revolution that General Lafayette was quoted as saying, "Whenever on the field I wanted a thing done well, I had a Butler do it." But besides the Butler bravery, he had also apparently inherited the stubborn streak for which the family was known and later gained notoriety for stubbornly resisting the famous "roundhead order" issued by General Wilkinson forbidding the wearing of a "queue," the long pigtail favored by Anglo aristocracy and colonial army officers. Court-martialled for insubordination by General James Wilkinson, he appealed to the Secretary of War. After much anguished correspondence with his dear friend Andrew Jackson, the colonel was still under order of courtmartial for resisting what he considered an "arbitrary infraction of his natural rights" when he perished of yellow fever in 1805 in New Orleans, and it was said a hole was cut in the bottom of his coffin so that his queue might hang out in defiance of "that damn scoundrel Wilkinson." It is his descendants we will follow henceforth.

Colonel Thomas' son Adjutant General Robert Butler was Chief of Staff (Aide-de-camp) to Andrew Jackson in the War of 1812 and Battle of New Orleans,

Another son of Colonel Thomas Butler was Judge Thomas Butler III, who was born in Pennsylvania in 1785 and died in 1847. In 1810 he moved south and was commissioned Captain of a Troop of Cavalry in Wilkinson County in the Militia of the Mississippi Territory by Governor Holmes. In late 1810 or early 1811, shortly after the West Florida Rebellion ousted the Spanish in the area, Judge Thomas Butler purchased lands along Alexander's Creek granted in the mid-1790s by Baron de Carondelet to John Allen and Patrick Holland. The early house was expanded in stages from 1795 to 1859. He married in 1813 Ann Madeline (Nancy) Ellis, who was born in 1794 and died in 1878; her parents were Margaret Gaillard and Abram Ellis of Laurel Hill Plantation near Natchez, Mississippi. It was through his marriage into this Ellis family that many of the possessions of Dr. William Newton Mercer, whose New Orleans home became the Boston Club, ended up at The Cottage and subsequently Butler Greenwood.

Judge Butler hosted Andrew Jackson at The Cottage when the general was on his way home to Tennessee after his victory at the Battle of New Orleans in 1815. A *Times-Picayune* article of 1939 says there were at least eight staff officers who were Butlers, including General Robert Butler, Jackson's chief of staff. In fact a number of Butler children married into the family of Andrew Jackson's wife Rachel (the Stokely/Donelson/Hays group) and some were even raised at The Hermitage by Jackson after the death of their parents. Judge Thomas Butler's siblings who married into Andrew Jackson's wife's family were Dr. William Edward Butler who married Patsy Hays, daughter of Robert Hays and Jane Donelson, niece of Rachel Jackson;

General Robert Butler who married Rachel Hays, daughter of Col. Robert Hays and Jane Donelson, niece of Rachel Jackson; and Lydia Butler who married Stokely Hays, nephew of Rachel Jackson.

Judge Thomas Butler was a loving husband and father, and much of his correspondence has been preserved at LSU. His letters, written on trips away from home on court business or while serving in Congress, often begin "My beloved wife" and end "Your fond husband," or "*Adieu* my dear Nannette, your most affectionate husband" and "Kiss my sweet children for me. How I long to see them and their dear mother, God bless you, Ever Yours."

He acquired several sugar cane plantations in Terrebonne Parish and cotton plantations in Louisiana and Mississippi (The Cottage was only about 300+ acres). He then served as the first judge of the Florida Parishes in 1812 after W.C.C. Claiborne claimed them for the United States and was a candidate for governor in 1824. Judge Butler was elected in 1818 to represent the area in the United State Congress, though he found in Washington "nothing like the agreeable social society we have in Louisiana."

And indeed the Judge had a comfortable and happy life at home at The Cottage, its name hinting at a rustic simplicity. Constructed long before the popularity of southern Greek Revival grandeur or Victorian flamboyance, the home instead exhibits a sensible sturdiness and for nearly 150 years it housed the sensible sturdy members of a single family.

Judge Thomas Butler's children (some of whom studied under Audubon's wife Lucy when she worked as tutor at the Percy plantation Beech Woods and the Garrett Johnson place) married into other plantation families. They included Percival who married Mary Louisa Stirling of Wakefield Plantation (daughter of Henry Stirling and Mary Bowman) and they lived at Ducro Plantation near Thibodaux until Mary Louisa died of consumption at age 23, when Pierce (Percival) and three children moved back to The Cottage, and among their children were a son Judge Thomas Butler of The Oaks Plantation who married Mary Fort (the daughter of William J. Fort of Catalpa Plantation and his wife, Sallie Jones Stewart, sister of Penelope Stewart Mathews of Butler Greenwood Plantation) and their children were Mary, Thomas, Sallie, William, Annie, Samuel, Henry Minor and James. A daughter of Percival and Mary Louisa Stirling was Anna Louise who married Henry Chotard Minor of Southdown Plantation in Houma and their daughter

Mary Louise Minor married David Washington Pipes, Jr., of Beech Grove Plantation in East Feliciana and they lived at Southdown Plantation and their children were David who died as a small child, Anna Fort Pipes who married Fenwick Eustis, Henry Minor Pipes who married Gifford Glenny, John Butler Pipes who married Virginia Lindsey, Katharine Minor Pipes who married Charles Mathews Butler, Mary Minor Pipes (- 1987) who married Robert Ormond Butler, and Margaret (Peggy) Gustine Pipes who married Howard Peabody.

The other children of Judge Thomas Butler III and Ann Madeline Ellis were Richard (whose son Thomas married Sallie Fort and their daughters were Sarah and Mamie Butler, spinsters whose home was The Cedars Plantation), and Dr. Robert Ormond Butler. Dr. Butler was born in 1832 and died in 1874, went to Yale and then studied medicine in Paris. He served as an important Civil War surgeon. In 1865 he married in Thibodaux Marguerite Burthe (? – 1880), and their children were Louise, spinster historian whose evocative works were published in historical quarterlies; Robert Ormond, bachelor; Marguerite who married Eugene Ellis and had children Amalie (Dinks), Marguerite (Geet) and Eleanor (Bea) Ellis; Margaret; Sarah; Anna; Mary Ellis; and Edward Gaillard (1871-1948) who graduated from Virginia Military Institute and in 1898 married Annie Mathews Lawrason(1878-1962).

During the Civil War, Capt. Thomas Butler was aide-de-camp to General Braxton Bragg, and Second Lieutenant James Pierce Butler was in the First Louisiana Heavy Artillery. Doctor Robert Ormond Butler was Surgeon in Chief under Brigadier General Pratt and wrote moving letters to his sister during the war. One, dated September 22, 1862, after having heard that Bayou Sara had been partially destroyed, said, "If I live fifty years I will never forget that midnight march down the river, it was one continued scene of desolation and sadness, nearly every place on the route had been...plundered even to the huts of the poorest creoles, the Mississippi once so teeming with life and gladness flowed by us as swiftly and silently as that stream which is said to flow to eternity...large plantations were deserted, not a living thing to be seen, the owners fled and the negroes carried off, these sights made our men furious and they vowed bitter vengeance on the villainous Yankees...At General Taylor's place the officers entered the house, it was a complete wreck, the furniture smashed, the walls torn down, pictures cut out of their frames while scattered over the floor lay the correspondence and official documents of the old General while President of the United States."

Dr. Butler's children and grandchildren were the last generations of Butlers to occupy The Cottage. His daughter Louise, who never married and lived at The Cottage with her unmarried brother Robert, was a writer and historian of some note, whose published pieces in early Louisiana Historical Quarterlies captured the very soul of southern plantation life in the nineteenth century. When The Cottage was sold by the Butler family in the 1950s, an effort was made to preserve other vivid images of life in the early days through the donation of priceless vintage books to the LSU Library, significant correspondence and records to the Louisiana and Lower Mississippi Valley Collection at LSU, and an incredible collection of early 19th-century garments to the university's Textile & Costume Museum. Even portions of the once-extensive gardens surrounding The Cottage were shared, with one enormous white azalea more than 100 feet in circumference shipped by railroad flatcar to Houston.

Today The Cottage, long and rambling, peacefully presides with unpretentious charm atop a bluff overlooking Alexander's Creek, a steel bridge now replacing the terrifying swinging bridge over the water; when the creek was running high in the early days, wagons and later autos could not cross to get out to the highway. A multitude of French doors open from the long front gallery admitting cooling breezes; the huge live oaks provide plenty of shade. To the rear, one of the state's most extensive and fascinating groupings of original plantation dependencies--the judge's office/schoolroom, smokehouse, saddle room, commissary, kitchen/laundry, dairy and well house, greenhouses, carriage house with Judge Butler's Philadelphia-made 1820 carriage, slave quarters used in filming *The Autobiography of Miss Jane Pittman*, brick-walled family cemetery--collectively provide a clear picture of life on functioning plantation communities of the early 19th century. Indeed, The Cottage has been called a state of mind, its antebellum ambience evoking the serenity of a bygone era.

THE SIXTH GENERATION

Charles Mathews Butler and his wife Katharine Minor Pipes Butler

The children of Annie Mathews Butler and Edward Gaillard Butler were: Edward Lawrason, Harriett Mathews (1901-1973), Charles Mathews(1910-1971), Robert Ormond (1919-)

Charles Mathews Butler was born in 1910, the last of the Butlers born at The Cottage Plantation, and died in 1970. He attended Julius Freyhan School in St. Francisville, travelling as a boy from The Cottage by train or by horse, as many of the students from outlying plantations did; there were stables on the school grounds. He always joked that he started public school in third grade because he was too big to fit into the 1st or 2nd grade desks, but no doubt he had been taught enough at home, where the library was voluminous and the parents well educated, that he could skip those early grades. He also attended Sewanee Military Academy in Tennessee, then graduated from LSU in 1932 with a BS in Civil Engineering.

He worked with the Corps of Engineers, US Army, specializing in hydrographic survey and dredging on the lower Mississippi River. On May 23, 1942, he enlisted and served until March 11, 1946, with the 842nd Engineer Aviation Battalion, 1113th Engineer Construction Group in the Pacific Theater. He spent World War II designing landing strips for McArthur's forces, serving in the battles and campaigns in the southern Philippines, New Guinea, Ryukyu Islands, and Bismarck Archipelago. He concluded his service with the rank of Major, earning the Asiatic-Pacific Campaign Medal with four bronze service stars, American Theater Campaign Medal, Philippine Liberation Ribbon with two bronze service stars, and the Victory Medal. His first child was born while he was overseas, and he carried a small leather folder with correspondence including the telegram announcing her birth and lots of baby pictures, as well as snapshots of various runways and bulldozers, foreign currency, and one awful image of several natives carrying a litter holding a severed human head.

After the war he worked briefly in Lake Charles, Louisiana, and in Vicksburg, Mississippi. He eventually began a private partnership with C. Carter Brown to form the consulting engineering firm of Brown & Butler in Baton Rouge, with his main interests being in the fields of air and marine terminal facilities and specialized studies and reports. An obituary in a national engineering publication said he was "a dedicated man and a credit to his profession. Thorough-going in all of his professional undertakings, his integrity was unquestioned and a matter of common knowledge. He was a quiet person of dignity, respected by all who knew him. His attributes were as equally evident in his personal life as in his professional career. Mr. Butler was a true professional in the accepted traditional sense of the word."

His wife, Katharine Minor Pipes, descended from the illustrious Minor family of Southdown Plantation in Terrebonne Parish, but had her own connections with the Butler line as well; her great-grandfather and her husband's grandfather were brothers, Percival and Robert Ormond Butler, sons of Judge Thomas Butler of The Cottage Plantation. She's shown here as a child in costume as Tom Thumb's Bride for a presentation.

The Minor (Miner) line begins, at least the record begins, in the 1300s with Henry Miner, a tin and silver miner supposedly awarded a coat of arms by King Edward III of England. Thomas Minor, born in 1608 in Chew Magna, England, came to America on the *Arabella* in 1629-30 with the company of Massachusetts Bay Colony founder John Winthrop St. and was one of the founders of Stonington, Connecticut; subsequent generations moved to Virginia and Pennsylvania.

Katharine Minor Pipes Butler's great-great-grandfather was Stephen Minor, born in 1760 in Greene County, Pennsylvania (then Virginia). He became one of the most influential foreigners in the Natchez District under Spanish rule and was named in 1797 as Gov. Manuel Gayosa de Lemos' successor to guide the transition to American power. Just about the entire town of Natchez, Mississippi, was built on land the Spanish government purchased from Stephen Minor.

Stephen Minor served the Spanish crown 1779-1807. At the young age of 19, he had descended the Mississippi River in 1779 bound for New Orleans with merchandise that was apparently a screen for obtaining war materials being supplied by Spain for American revolutionaries in the West. He joined the royal Spanish army being assembled by Louisiana governor Bernardo de Galvez in attacking English forces with Spanish and American troops under Galvez's command, in return for which he was accorded the rank of captain and granted the land on which Natchez was built.

In 1781 Galvez appointed Minor adjutant of the military post at Natchez commanded by Manuel Gayoso de Lemos (whose personal physician was Dr. Samuel Flower). He served as liaison between Spanish officials and the Anglo-American settlers and Natchez Indians, and was known as *Don Esteban*. After the creation of the Mississippi Territory by the US Congress, Spain ceded power to the United States, and the Spanish evacuated Natchez in 1798. Minor acquired Concord Plantation, built in 1794, from Gayosa de Lemos and succeeded de Lemos as Governor of the Natchez District. He died at majestic Concord in Natchez in 1815.

Stephen Minor was a planter, cattleman, and great horse racing enthusiast as well as early president of the Bank of Mississippi. He had plantations in Adams County of Mississippi producing tobacco, indigo and cotton, and about 40,000 acres east of the Pearl River in Louisiana. He married first a Miss Bingaman of Natchez. His second wife was Martha Ellis, daughter of Richard Ellis and wife Mary Cocke, and their children included Mary Minor who married William Kenner and they were the parents of Duncan F. Kenner, distinguished sugar planter and legislator of Ashland-Belle Helene Plantation on Louisiana's rich River Road, which explains why the Kenners evacuated to Mary Minor Kenner's brother's home at Southdown Plantation in Terrebonne Parish when Union troops were sacking River Road plantations. Thirdly Stephen Minor married Katharine Lintot, born in 1770 in Pennsylvania, sister of Fanny Lintot whose husband Philip Nolan lost his life on an illegal horse hunting expedition in Texas in 1797; see *Man Without A Country*. The children of Stephen Minor by his third marriage to Katharine Lintot were Frances who married Major Henry Chotard, William John who married Rebecca Gustine, Stephen and Katharine. His wife Katharine was known as the Yellow Duchess for her fondness for things golden.

Stephen Minor's son William John Minor was born in 1808 at Concord in Natchez but educated at the University of Pennsylvania; his wife Rebecca Ann Gustine was born in 1813 and died in 1887. In 1828 he purchased a 1790s Spanish land grant property briefly owned by Jim and Rezin Bowie in Terrebonne Parish on Little Bayou Black. He added to the initial grant until he had more than 10,000 acres of prime fields, planted first in indigo and then ribbon cane as the market for domestic sugar increased. The introduction of steam mills combined with improved techniques of manufacturing granulated sugar to begin a boom period for the industry. He started production on Southdown Plantation in 1831 with a yield of 36 hogsheads of sugar and 15 years later constructed his own steam-powered cane mill capable of processing his annual output, then ranging between 40,000 and 50,000 gallons. In 1853 the plantation yield was up to 937 hogsheads of sugar, and an on-site sawmill provided lumber for mill repairs. There were 176 slaves living on Southdown by the 1850s.

In 1858 William Minor began construction of the Southdown house for his family which included nine children, all but one of them boys. It was a single-story Greek Revival structure originally with two-story wings at each end surrounding a courtyard; later it would be enlarged with a second story flanked by two-story rounded turrets. Bricks were made in his own kilns and cypress from his swamps was finished in his own sawmill; possibly it was the Civil War that had prevented the second story being completed initially. Solid brick walls were nearly two feet thick, ceilings were 14 feet, with 11-inch-thick doorways off the broad arched entrance hall into downstairs rooms: library, bedrooms, breakfast room, turret-topped parlor with curved walls. The double front entrance doors featured stained glass panels with sugar cane scenes. Upstairs were six more bedrooms and a sitting room. There were double front galleries, plus additional porches on the sides and rear of the house. A two-story brick structure behind the main house, originally attached by covered walkway, was part of the slave quarters built in the late 1840s.

He was a racing enthusiast and had extensive stables full of fine horses, as well as his own railroad lines and bayou barges to transport his cane from field to mill. William J. Minor and his wife opposed the war, but one son Duncan was killed fighting for the Confederacy in Virginia and another son Stephen contracted typhoid fever in a Confederate camp in Kentucky and died young. The house is now a museum and has been painted pink and green, which the last generations of the Minor/Pipes family to live there insist was never the color; it was always white with green shutters.

When William J. Minor died in 1869, his son Henry Chotard Minor and unmarried daughter Katharine (Kate) Minor (1846-1923) bought out the interests of the other brothers. In 1893 they enclosed the courtyard and added a second story between the towering rounded turrets as Southdown embraced the more flamboyant Victorian style then in vogue. In 1875 Henry Chotard Minor married Anna Louise Butler (1843-1906) at her home The Cottage Plantation in West Feliciana Parish; only three of their six children survived infancy. The youngest, Mary Louise Minor, was orphaned as a fairly young girl and was raised at Southdown by her aunt Kate, who was an active participant in running the sugar plantation. This was considered a rarity at the time, a woman engaged in agricultural management, but actually there were many strong and capable women in the South, particularly after the Civil War; large numbers of men did not survive the war years, and those who lived through the battles came home so disabled or despondent that their wives and mothers were forced to continue in demanding roles assumed when their husbands and sons and fathers had been away fighting. Kate Minor was one of the Louisiana commissioners to the 1893 World's Columbian Exposition.

Mary Louise Minor was born in 1886 and graduated from Newcomb prior to marrying in 1910 David Washington Pipes, Jr. She would live until 1961, when she collapsed while shopping in New Orleans.

Her husband, also born in 1886, outlived her by seven years. He was a graduate of Washington & Lee University in Virginia and received a law degree from Tulane University. His father David Washington Pipes (1845-1939) was born on the Pipes family place in East Feliciana Parish called Beech Grove Plantation, and married first Ella V. Norwood and second Anna Thornton Key Fort(1861-1948), the daughter of William Johnston Fort (1861-1948) and his wife Sallie Jones Stewart (1826-1914) of Holly Grove Plantation and Catalpa Plantation; Sallie Stewart was the sister of Butler Greenwood Plantation's Penelope Stewart Mathews. His grandfather Windsor Pipes was in Natchez by 1780, and in fact was one of the patrons of the mercantile business operated by Richard Carpenter.

His recorded recollections of fighting in the Civil War with the famed Washington Artillery, a 17-year-old taking his slave with him, provide a fascinating historical memoir. Famed Louisiana author Harnett T. Kane interviewed him when he was 94 and had moved to the Garden District in New Orleans, calling him the last War Between the States survivor of the famed Washington Artillery, the only living son of an officer in the Battle of New Orleans, former state senator and representative, member of the Constitutional Convention of 1898. He told Harnett Kane he was "probably the only veteran of the war who went in a private of the rear ranks and came out one, and remained one ever since," although he narrowly escaped death many times and had horses killed under him. When he returned from the war to a ruined country of poverty and distress, he "turned to the soil, and through the rest of my life I've been first of all a farmer." In later years he became a successful businessman in New Orleans, owning interests in railroads, coffee companies, electric companies, banks and plantations. David W. Pipes, who died in 1939, and his father

David Pipes, who was born in 1789, between them lived under the administration of every American president from George Washington to Franklin D. Roosevelt, according to *Ripley's Believe It Or Not!*

Mary Minor Pipes and her husband David Washington Pipes, Jr. (called the "Father of Sugar"), lived in the main house on Southdown Plantation. Along with her sister Margaret Minor and husband Charles C. Krumbhaar, they supervised the extensive sugar operations at Southdown, increased land holdings to some 20,000 acres, and installed a modern sugar mill capable of producing 2,000 tons of sugar daily. When the industry was threatened by mosaic disease, root rot and recurrent hurricanes, they established a U.S. Department of Agriculture sugarcane experiment station at Southdown and imported a hardy, disease-resistant POJ strain of cane from Java, generously sharing seedlings with other planters to save the cane industry in Louisiana. Southdown was also the first to introduce a practical utilization of bagasse, sugar cane's previously wasted fibrous by-product, for the manufacture of building board, as well as the carbon filtration process of juice purification.

During the Depression in the 1930s, Canal Bank foreclosed on a mortgage of Southdown Plantation prior to the end of grinding season, which was of questionable legality, and the family moved into a large home that had been Aunt Kate's connected to the overseer's house.

The Pipes family included four daughters: Anna Fort Pipes called Nan, 1914-1985; Katharine, 1922-1982; Mary Minor, born in 1925; and Margaret called Peggy, born in 1927; plus three sons, David who was born in 1912 and died two years later, most likely from ruptured appendix; Henry Minor, 1916-1984; and John Butler, born in 1919. Two of the daughters married into the Butler family of their grandmother from The

Cottage. Katharine Minor Pipes went to Newcomb and LSU, then became a licensed pilot during World War II hoping to ferry planes across the sea, meeting the height requirements for pilot training by stuffing her hairdo with cotton. She married Charles Mathews Butler, and her younger sister Mary Minor Pipes married his younger brother Robert Ormond Butler.

Charles Mathews Butler and Katharine Minor Pipes Butler had two children, Anne Lawrason Butler (me) and Mary Minor Butler. Anne L. Butler has two children, Chase Mathews Poindexter who married Steven Cunningham, and Charles Stewart Hamilton III who married Laura Metz and has two sons, John Stewart Hamilton and Carter Lewis Hamilton. Mary Minor Butler married Paul Michael Hebert, and they have two children, Elizabeth (Betsy) and Anne, and three grandchildren.

While the Great Depression of the 1930s played out in different ways in different places, causing one part of the family to lose their sugar plantation in Terrebonne Parish of Louisiana and another part of the family to hold on to their plantation in West Feliciana Parish, an entirely different scenario was playing out in Natchez, Mississippi. There, Stephen Minor's courtly grandson Duncan Minor, who bore a startling resemblance to Clark Gable in his prime, became embroiled in the famous Goat Castle Murder of 1932, a time when many members of prominent Natchez families had fallen into secluded lifestyles noted more for eccentricity than elegance. At age 69 he was considered one of the wealthiest men in town, but was noted for such parsimonious behavior his cook had to hold an umbrella over her head while preparing meals in rainy weather. At a time when most others drove automobiles, he sat erect in the saddle, white-haired and white-mustached, when he faithfully arrived on horseback each evening for more than 30 years to pay his respects to his beloved second cousin Jane Surget Merrill of Glenburnie.

An aristocratic and wealthy spinster raised abroad when her father was ambassador to Belgium, presented at the Court of St. James, she clung to outdated styles herself, hoarded her money, and received only one caller, her beloved Duncan Minor, who would discover her bloody body when he arrived for his customary evening call on August 4, 1932. The finger of guilt initially pointed next door to Glenwood, deteriorating home of concert pianist Dick Dana and writer Octavia Dockery, where hard times and deprivation had driven the occupants to near-insanity, goats and chickens running loose in the house, no running water, sparse meals cooked in the marble-manteled drawing rom fireplace, and an animosity toward Miss Jennie Merrill who had shot several goats straying onto her property. As the sensationalized Goat Castle Murder would play out in print around the world, the Glenwood occupants were finally exonerated and would turn their notoriety into a most unusual tour through the famous falling-down mansion, enhanced by piano concerts by Dick Dana in white linen suit and poetry readings by Miss Dockery.

THE SEVENTH GENERATION

Anne Lawrason Butler

The children of Charles Mathews Butler and Katharine Minor Pipes Butler were: Anne Lawrason Butler (1944-) and Mary Minor Butler (1946-)

Anne Lawrason Butler, that's me, born in 1944, writer, Bed and Breakfast operator, historic tour guide and avid preservationist. I'm the author of more than twenty books, some more substantial than others, but most preserving the history and culture of Louisiana as well as books on true crime, humor, travel, cookbooks and children's books, plus hundreds of articles for newspapers and magazines. My children used to laugh when told how lucky they were to have a famous cookbook author as their mother; truth be told, I really don't cook much, and my cookbooks are more history books, with stories of families and old houses, the recipes given provenance like antiques. Food just tastes better for knowing who first cooked it and where it was served, the traditional dishes becoming almost like treasured family members. I donate my time and talents as publicist for all manner of non-profits ranging from the historical society's pilgrimage to the animal shelter's annual fund-raising gala (come smooch a pooch), and in this little country town I'm in great demand as the local obituary writer; I can make anybody sound good, although some require more effort than others.

I first married Virginia-born Miles Poindexter III (1945-) and our child was Chase Mathews Poindexter, born in 1975, who married Steven Cunningham. Second husband was Glenn Daniel; we had no children. Third husband was Charles Stewart Hamilton, Jr., and our son Charles Stewart Hamilton III was born in 1985 and married Laura Metz, and they have two sons, John Stewart Hamilton and Carter Lewis Hamilton. Last husband was C. Murray Henderson (deceased) about whom the less said the better. My tombstone epitaph should read (stolen from some book): *She Flung Herself Eagerly Into The Paths Of Unsuitable Men.*

I was born during World War II while my father was overseas, so my mother and I spent time living with both sets of grandparents, in St. Francisville and in Houma, until he came home. I always loved my Greenwood grandmother, for whom I was named and looked like. My father was a consulting engineer in Baton Rouge, and a longterm consulting job in England allowed us all to travel through Europe and back home on the *Queen Mary*, quite an experience for an elementary school student.

This of course was before desegregation, and it wasn't until I finally saw the movie *The Help* that it struck me why there was a separate bathroom in our carport, and why my mother kept the plate on which she served the yardman his lunch under the kitchen sink. Baton Rouge neighborhoods were pretty much separated by race, whereas in the country around Greenwood, everyone lived in closer proximity and relations somehow seemed to be more respectful; perhaps it was the result of knowing different types of people just as people rather than some unknown entity, knowing their mama, knowing their grandma. Maybe.

Beginning in junior high, I attended University High where all the LSU student teachers practiced. It was a very good semi-private school right on the LSU campus. After graduating in 1961, I went to Sweet Briar College in Virginia, majored in English with a minor in Psychology, and graduated in three years by attending summer sessions at University of Wisconsin-Madison and also at LSU. Academically Sweet Briar was a fine school, and it was a beautiful hilly wooded campus. I lived for weekends away at University of Virginia in Charlottesville or Washington & Lee in Lexington, where I dated the captain of the football and baseball teams and was actually on the homecoming court.

After graduation I went to Washington, D.C.; had no job, no place to live, just got on the train and went. I lived in a beautiful rowhouse in Georgetown with female roommates and worked at the America Automobile Association writing tour guides. This entailed some travelling for AAA. I had been in San Francisco and Los Angeles writing AAA Citibooks and flew back into D.C. the night Martin Luther King was killed, and it was terrifying to see smoke rising from burning buildings from the air. The AAA building was just around the corner from the White House, and the next day, all the women were sent home and told to stay inside. I took some time off to spend six weeks in Spain travelling around the country on my own. Main claim to fame in D.C.: dated Denny Doherty, later of the *Mamas and Papas*, charming Canadian with that wonderful voice (*Monday Monday*).

In 1968 at age 24 I married a friend from college, Miles Poindexter III, and we spent a couple of years living on the Monterey Peninsula in California, a beautiful coastal area back before Cannery Row became so touristy and was more as Steinbeck memorialized it, with Doc's studio not even locked, and one of the houses we rented had been built of driftwood by the author himself; another had gorgeous purple fuchsia vines growing all over the tile roof. I was writing for local magazines and newspapers in the Carmel/Big Sur area, interviewing artists and writers and celebrities like Jackie Robinson who was in town while the famous golf tournament was going on at Pebble Beach, and when I asked if he were playing in it, he replied that they didn't allow blacks there.

We moved to northern California in the redwood country and I earned an MA in English at Humboldt State in 1970, then returned to Greenwood, my grandmother and father both having died. I have lived here and put every penny I could earn into restoring and maintaining the house and grounds for 50 years.

It was kind of a culture shock, me a radical liberal moving to a very conservative small town; I must have been the only local white person who voted for George McGovern for president. I worked a few years as the Old Age worker in the local welfare department, then founded and ran the Council on Aging, treating black and white clients with the same respect. When the CoA needed an office, there was a problem finding a facility that would accept integrated services, so I provided a little cabin on Butler Greenwood frontage to serve in that capacity. We provided meals, transportation, educational programs and lots more, and it was all greatly appreciated because there had been no resources whatsoever before.

My daughter Chase was in elementary school during most of my years at the CoA, and I found that my elderly country clients were operating at the same level of social deprivation as Chase's class, so when the kindergartners went to the zoo or the planetarium, for example, I took my old folks there, too, and they absolutely loved those experiences they had missed as children. One Christmas we had a party complete with a wonderful old black Santa Claus in full regalia. When a very dignified and well-dressed white lady arrived to donate dolls for clients to give their grandchildren, Santa said, "Hey babydoll, come sit on my lap and tell me what you want me to bring you." I held my breath. She went right over, sat in his lap, and said, "I want a Lincoln Continental and a good man." And his reply was, "I'll work on the Lincoln. I'm out of the man business!"

These old folks had lived close to the land, farming and working cattle; they had little formal education. Most were required to work in the fields at harvest time and thus were not able to go much higher than elementary grades in the little black schools scattered around the rural areas that taught utilitarian skills like using cornshucks to make doormats and mule collars. But they were some of the smartest people I'd ever met. When the welfare office opened a little craft shop, the colorful quilts considered strictly utilitarian were suddenly appreciated as art. During one pilgrimage we had all of these crafts and also fresh produce on sale, and one old farmer arrived bearing yard eggs, all dressed to the nines in his best suit. I took him aside and said, "Mathew, this is supposed to be kinda old-timey. Do you think you have anything else you might wear?" And so he answered, "Oh, I getcha. Come in *costume!*" And the next day he arrived in threadbare overalls and an old straw hat that looked like it had been run over in the road, and of course he sold all of his eggs!

For the most part, the historic properties and tourist-related businesses have worked together to promote our charming little country destination, cooperating with advertising, referring overflow guests to other facilities, sharing promotional costs and community activities. Right after the 9-11 terrorist attacks, we all got together and thought about what we could do to help; we decided what we did best was to offer hospitality, to soothe the soul, and so we offered a week's respite from the horror, with everything free for one of the first responders--- free lodging, free food, free tours, free recreation, free car, and a July 4th parade of all fire trucks since our recipient was a young firefighter and his wife; they loved it.

Sometimes I feel like Scarlett O'Hara, not for her frivolous southern belle-ism, but for her faith in the land, something I could always count on. For fifty years I have taken a good bit of my identity from this old place. Living in a historic house is not for the fainthearted; it's a bottomless pit, with always a long list of things waiting to be done, freezing in winter, requiring endless maintenance work and enormous expense, but you can't let it overwhelm you.

It's necessary to let these old places help support themselves. After years of saying "never never never," I did finally open the house for guided tours and then for Bed & Breakfast in cottages on the grounds, some of them historic dependencies and others newly built. I personally conducted tours through the house every day from 9 to 5, and it was a bit unusual for a member of the original family to be doing that and maybe added a little warmth and personal stories. After 23 years I finally had had just about all the joys of dealing with the travelling American public that I could stand, so to save my sanity I stopped doing tours in 2014 and just continue offering overnight accommodations in the cottages. As a writer, the minute I would sit down at the computer, the first ten interruptions I was polite, the second ten I was what Miss Lucy Parlange would call *marginally civil,* and the last ten I was about to blow my top.

I always looked for something different to write about. Living in the country, there were not many jobs, but working as a welfare Old-Age worker and Council on Aging director, I found the inspiration for many articles. And even with full-time jobs, I kept on writing, articles for the Baton Rouge newspapers and area magazines, children's books, humor, preservation and history, travel/tour books, even cookbooks that are history books in disguise. Famous chef John Folse, a friend who has filmed at Butler Greenwood Plantation and invited me to appear on his television shows many times, for years would ask me to give a lecture to his culinary classes at Nicholls State University on English cooking as he tried to show the various cultural and ethnic influences on Louisiana cuisine. I'd say, "John, you *know* I can't cook," and he'd respond, "Well, you can *talk,* can't you?" And yes, I can talk. And write.

When my last husband tried to kill me when I began divorce proceedings, shooting me five times at point-blank range with a .38, I would make something worthwhile out of the two years' worth of surgeries and therapy by writing a book that I hope gave a voice to what had in the past been mostly a silent crime, the victims too afraid or too inarticulate or lacking a venue to speak up. I did a lot of public speaking on domestic violence, everywhere from the New York State Supreme Court to anger-management classes at state prisons, and my message always was: "You do not have the right to kill somebody. If you don't like them, get away." I am not sure how we have lost our communication skills to the extent that we must solve our problems with guns or knives instead of verbally. And the other part of my message: "If you're gonna shoot somebody, don't shoot a writer;" you'll get your just deserts when the book comes out.

I named my book after the epitaph on a little 1830's baby's gravestone: "Stranger if e'er these lines be read, Weep for the living, not the dead." The opening line of *Weep For The Living* was "I have been carried in the arms of angels," and I believed I had been. I was contacted by a psychic who said she had seen the whole tragedy in a dream, and she wanted to paint a picture of me with angels, so I told her my two main angels were Rose Pate, who had worked with me for many years and who spent months standing in front of me and shielding me if anyone came through the door before the perpetrator was finally jailed, and Burnett Carraway. Both posed with me for the artist. Weren't they surprised when they were depicted in the finished painting as two blonde-haired white female angels; Rose is black and Burnett is male. I took Rose with me for an appearance on the *Montel* television show in New York to promote book sales, and Rose, who would talk to a tree, was struck dumb the minute her hero Montel asked her a question on live TV.

Throughout all these years, my rock has been Burnett Carraway, Mississippi master carpenter who shared with me a deep appreciation and understanding of this old house and what it needed. He knew how to do everything and how to do it properly, and he did it. He restored the main house and especially the parlor when the ceiling fell in, restored the 1850s garden gazebo which unfortunately later was crushed by falling trees in the 2016 flood, restored the two historic dependencies used as B&Bs and built the six new ones without the first blueprint or plan. He just loved this place and put his heart and soul into it, and then one day he looked at me and said, "You must know I love you, too.

I've loved you for years." We had always planned to make this his last retirement job, spending a couple of days a week here and then having the rest of the time to do his church work as Baptist minister near his home in little Smithdale, Mississippi.

For years we shared a deep and complex relationship, a gratifying sense of continuity, and finally after we were both free, we were trying to figure out how to satisfactorily combine two separate lives in different states full of inescapable responsibilities without compromising his calling. We were looking forward to growing old together, but I guess we didn't recognize that we already *were* old. For so many years Burnett carried such a heavy load for so many people, and even with his great big heart, it was just too much; he had a heart attack and stroke, and died on February 16, 2018.

He had a deep and abiding faith and looked forward to rejoicing in God's presence free of pain and care. One look at those gnarled hands and battered knuckles crossed over his chest in his coffin, and you knew he was a builder, a planter of seeds, a creator, a savior of old and lost things. He was proud to have been a master carpenter like Jesus, and he could work miracles with tired old structures; he worked just as many miracles saving lost souls. Like me. It would be easy to give up now without his help, but I look on this as continuing his legacy and mine as well, carrying on and joining the long line of lone strong women who kept this old place going.

THE EIGHTH GENERATION

Chase Mathews Poindexter and her husband Steven Cunningham; Charles Stewart Hamilton III and his wife Laura Metz Hamilton.

The children of Anne Lawrason Butler are:

Chase Mathews Poindexter (1975-) and Charles Stewart Hamilton III (1985-)

Talk about a strong survivor. The best description of my beautiful little drama-queen daughter Chase is this: Though she be but little, she is fierce. This has been true all of her life, for she has been plagued by physical problems since she was diagnosed with Type I Diabetes at age 9. And yet she is brave and driven, self-motivated to excel. She was named the student of the year for the entire parish in high school and was Salutatorian at graduation, went off to Oxford in Georgia for two years and then graduated from Emory University on the Dean's List in spite of receiving the shocking news of my shooting as she moved into her dorm for her senior year.

She worked as an *au pair* in Lyon, France, for a year, travelled around Europe, then worked in Washington, D.C., as a paralegal, eventually returning to Louisiana to work in state government at the office of Culture, Recreation and Tourism in Baton Rouge near the capitol. She endured dialysis treatments three times weekly for a year when her kidneys failed, and then miraculously received a double transplant, both kidney and pancreas, at Ochsner Hospital in New Orleans. In tribute to the deceased young donor of her lifesaving organs, she participated in the swimming events one year at the international Transplant Olympics. Now she has married and moved to Hattiesburg, Mississippi, with her nice laid-back husband Steven Cunningham, their family completed by two cat children.

My son Stewart graduated from high school, went to Nicholls State University for a year and had so much fun being a KA down in Cajun Country that he couldn't spare much energy for studying. He transferred to Delgado in New Orleans to get his degree. Then he married his high school sweetheart Laura Metz, an LSU grad from a well-respected old logging family in West Feliciana. Their wedding was a beautiful romantic one on the front lawn under the live oaks, with Burnett officiating, and a reception blow-out under a tent in the back yard complete with dance floor and band. Laura is lovely and talented, a great chef and creative artist.

Both have fulltime jobs, Stewart at the parish tax assessor's office and Laura managing a pediatric practice. Stewart coaches athletic teams for their two young sons, John Stewart and Carter, starting at the T-ball age when half the players are lying on the field on their backs watching the clouds with their legs up in the air and the others are wandering off to use the bathroom; he shows tremendous patience with these tiny ballplayers and actually manages to impart some lessons in sportsmanship and skill. It is good that he takes after his father, a cattleman and school-bus driver who absolutely loved all the little children of several generations (60 years of busloads of shrieking children and it was probably a good thing he was a little bit deaf), a hard worker who was never too busy to help anyone in need.

THE NINTH GENERATION

John Stewart Hamilton and Carter Lewis Hamilton

The children of Charles Stewart Hamilton III and his wife Laura Metz are:

John Stewart Hamilton and Carter Lewis Hamilton.

The boys and their parents will have to write their own stories, these last two generations on the place. Hopefully there will be many more in this remarkable family.

#

AFTERWORD

I had always known what a fine carpenter and eloquent preacher he was, but I had not expected Burnett to give me some of the most valuable literary criticism I ever received. A voracious reader, he especially loved Louis L'Amour's early western tales, had an enormous collection of his books, and read them over and over. And he always told me, "Remember what Louis L'Amour does. There's always an Indian hiding behind the next rock, or just over the next hilltop." Keep the reader's interest up. I figure Burnett is looking over this effort as well and his advice applies even to this family history, for as his hero Louis L'Amour said, no memory is ever alone; it's at the end of a trail of memories, a dozen trails that each have their own associations. Lord knows this history has many trails, many memories, and hopefully something unexpected behind every rock to keep the reader reading on, even if the Indian turns out to be a fierce and bloodied Anglo warrior.

I've always resisted genealogy and organizations like the DAR; stand on your own feet, I've always said, not your grandma's. But those words of Tolkien's poem resonate, even more than the famous line about not all who wander are lost, now seen on everything from wall plaques to t-shirts. Here's my favorite: the old that is strong does not wither; deep roots are not reached by the frost.

And so, after every hurricane, I look out on devastated lawns full of fallen trees, the pond laced with shattered branches, and I think to myself I'm not the first to do this and hopefully I won't be the last. Then I remember all of the generations of strong women, many of them widows, who struggled and showed what great courage and determination they had, and like them, I roll up my sleeves and start cleaning up and moving on

Lightning Source UK Ltd.
Milton Keynes UK
UKHW04n2059310718
326589UK00001B/1/P